# MACHINES CLOSE-UP

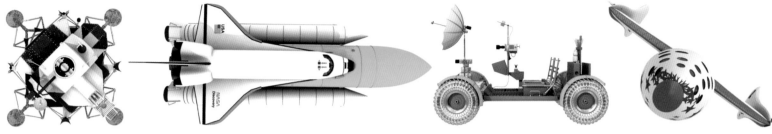

# SPACECRAFT

## Daniel Gilpin and Alex Pang

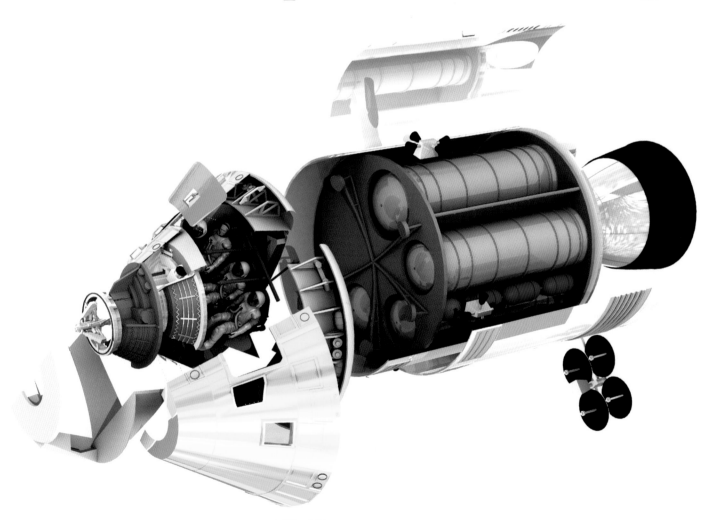

**Marshall Cavendish**
Benchmark

New York

This edition first published in 2011 in the United States by
Marshall Cavendish Benchmark

An imprint of Marshall Cavendish Corporation

Website: www.marshallcavendish.us

This publication represents the opinions and views of the author based on
Daniel Gilpin's and Alex Pang's personal experience, knowledge, and
research. The information in this book serves as a general guide only. The
author and publisher have used their best efforts in preparing this book and
disclaim liability rising directly and indirectly from the use and application of
this book.

Other Marshall Cavendish Offices:
Marshall Cavendish International (Asia) Private Limited, 1 New Industrial
Road, Singapore 536196 • Marshall Cavendish International (Thailand) Co
Ltd. 253 Asoke, 12th Flr, Sukhumvit 21 Road, Klongtoey Nua, Wattana,
Bangkok 10110, Thailand • Marshall Cavendish (Malaysia) Sdn Bhd, Times
Subang, Lot 46, Subang Hi-Tech Industrial Park, Batu Tiga, 40000 Shah
Alam, Selangor Darul Ehsan, Malaysia

Marshall Cavendish is a trademark of Times Publishing Limited

Copyright © 2009 David West Children's Books

Library of Congress Cataloging-in-Publication Data

Gilpin, Daniel.
Spacecraft / Daniel Gilpin and Alex Pang.
p. cm. -- (Machines close-up)
Includes index.
Summary: "Reveals and discusses the intricate internal workings of
spacecrafts"--Provided by publisher.
ISBN 978-1-60870-112-4
1. Space vehicles--Juvenile literature. I. Pang, Alex. II. Title.

TL793.G477 2011
629.47--dc22

2009045045

First published in 2009 by Wayland
Hachette Children's Books
338 Euston Road
London NW1 3BH
Wayland Australia
Level 17/207 Kent Street
Sydney, NSW 2000

Produced by
David West 🏃 Children's Books
7 Princeton Court
55 Felsham Road
London SW15 1AZ

Editor: Katharine Pethick
Designer: Gary Jeffrey
Illustrator: Alex Pang
Consultant: Steve Parker

The photographs in this book are used by permission and through the
courtesy of:

Abbreviations: t-top, m-middle, b-bottom, r-right,
l-left, c-center.
4-9 all images courtesy of NASA except 6tl,
Retromoderns; 7tl, p_a_h; 30 all images courtesy of
NASA

Printed in China
135642

# CONTENTS

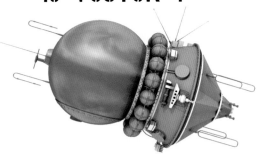

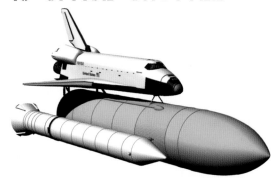
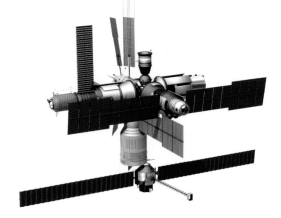
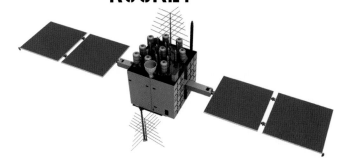

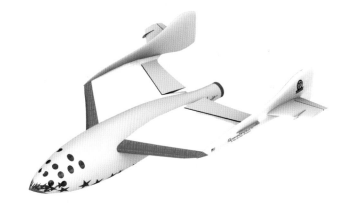
Glossary Words: when a word is printed in **bold**, you can look up its meaning in the Glossary on page 31.

# INTRODUCTION

Not so long ago spacecraft were science fiction. Today they have a great effect on our lives. Without them there would be no satellite TV, Global Positioning System (GPS), or hurricane warnings. Future spacecraft may affect us even more.

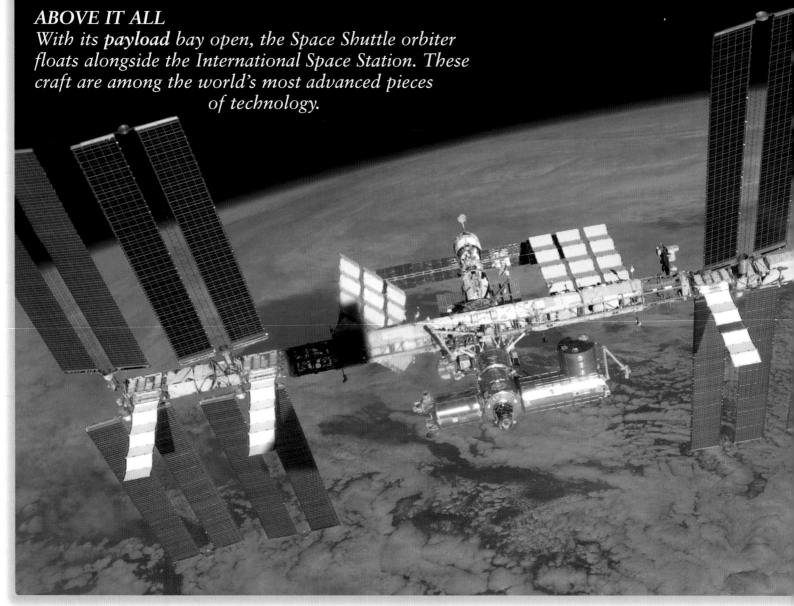

*ABOVE IT ALL*
*With its **payload** bay open, the Space Shuttle orbiter floats alongside the International Space Station. These craft are among the world's most advanced pieces of technology.*

# HOW TO USE THIS BOOK

## SPECIFICATIONS

Gives information about the vehicle's capacity and dimensions.

## MAIN TEXT

Explains the function of the spacecraft and outlines the history of its use. Other information, such as which nations developed the vehicle, is also covered here.

## INTERESTING FEATURES

Contains text and illustrations explaining how the vehicle works. Alternatively, this section may look in greater detail at one aspect of the vehicle or its mission.

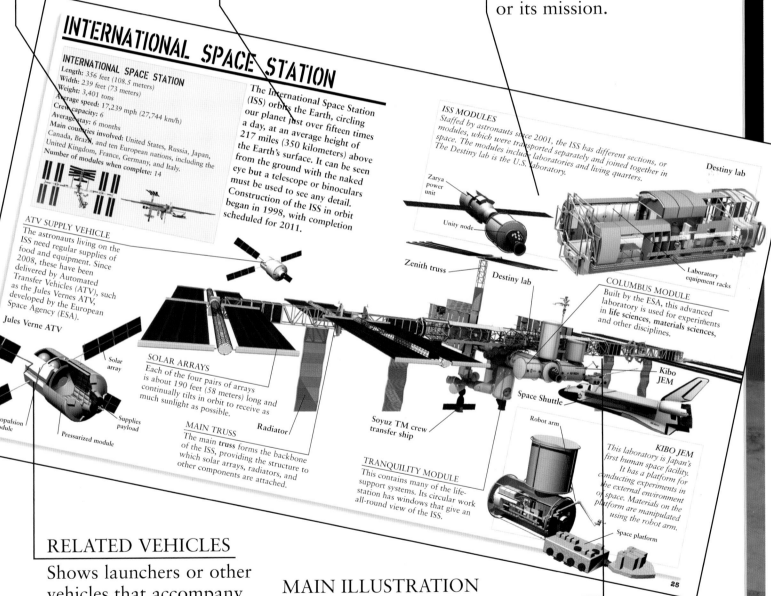

### INTERNATIONAL SPACE STATION

**INTERNATIONAL SPACE STATION**
Length: 356 feet (108.5 meters)
Width: 239 feet (73 meters)
Weight: 3,401 tons
Average speed: 17,239 mph (27,744 km/h)
Crew capacity: 6
Average stay: 6 months
Main countries involved: United States, Russia, Japan, Canada, Brazil, and ten European nations, including the United Kingdom, France, Germany, and Italy.
Number of modules when complete: 14

The International Space Station (ISS) orbits the Earth, circling our planet just over fifteen times a day, at an average height of 217 miles (350 kilometers) above the Earth's surface. It can be seen from the ground with the naked eye but a telescope or binoculars must be used to see any detail. Construction of the ISS in orbit began in 1998, with completion scheduled for 2011.

**ATV SUPPLY VEHICLE**
The astronauts living on the ISS need regular supplies of food and equipment. Since 2008, these have been delivered by Automated Transfer Vehicles (ATV), such as the Jules Vernes ATV, developed by the European Space Agency (ESA).

Jules Verne ATV

Propulsion module
Pressurized module
Solar array
Supplies payload

**SOLAR ARRAYS**
Each of the four pairs of arrays is about 190 feet (58 meters) long and continually tilts in orbit to receive as much sunlight as possible.

**MAIN TRUSS**
The main truss forms the backbone of the ISS, providing the structure to which solar arrays, radiators, and other components are attached.

Radiator

Soyuz TM crew transfer ship

**TRANQUILITY MODULE**
This contains many of the life-support systems. Its circular work-station has windows that give an all-round view of the ISS.

**ISS MODULES**
Staffed by astronauts since 2001, the ISS has different sections, or modules, which were transported separately and joined together in space. The modules include laboratories and living quarters. The Destiny lab is the U.S. laboratory.

Zarya power unit
Unity node
Zenith truss
Destiny lab
Laboratory equipment racks

**COLUMBUS MODULE**
Built by the ESA, this advanced laboratory is used for experiments in life sciences, materials sciences, and other disciplines.

Space Shuttle
Kibo JEM
Robot arm

**KIBO JEM**
This laboratory is Japan's first human space facility. It has a platform for conducting experiments in the external environment of space. Materials on the platform are manipulated using the robot arm.

Space platform

## RELATED VEHICLES

Shows launchers or other vehicles that accompany the main vehicle. Alternatively, this section may show a similar spacecraft.

## MAIN ILLUSTRATION

Shows the internal structure of the spacecraft and gives information on the positions of its various working parts.

# BREAKING BARRIERS

**I**n the early twentieth century, spaceflight was only a distant dream. During World War II, however, developments in rocket science led to space travel becoming a reality.

*BELL X-1*
*In 1947, this American rocket ship was the first to fly faster than the speed of sound—an important stage in the race into space.*

*A-4 ROCKET*
*Also known as the V-2, this was the world's first ballistic missile and the forerunner of all modern rockets.*

### FIRST SPACECRAFT

Spaceflight began in 1944, when a German A-4 rocket left the atmosphere before falling back to Earth. The A-4 was not actually designed to be a space vehicle. The first real spacecraft were developed in the former **Soviet Union**.

*SPUTNIK 1*
*In 1957 this unmanned Soviet craft became the first artificial satellite to orbit the Earth. The launch of Sputnik 1 alarmed the U.S. government and sparked the beginning of the "Space Race."*

*EXPLORER 1*
*The first U.S. satellite*

### PASSENGERS

Following the success of Sputnik 1, plans were made to put a man in orbit. The first creature to orbit the Earth was a dog called Laika. In 1957, she went into space aboard Sputnik 2, but died during the mission.

*FIRST ASTRONAUT*
*Yuri Gagarin was the first man in space. He orbited the Earth aboard the Soviet craft Vostok 1 in April 1961.*

## CIRCLING THE EARTH

After Laika, the Soviets sent several more dogs into orbit while the technology for successful human spaceflight was perfected. In 1961, Yuri Gagarin orbited the Earth, spending more than an hour in space before **reentry**.

### MERCURY CAPSULE

*Mercury was America's answer to Vostok 1. In 1962, it succeeded in putting a man into orbit.*

### JOHN GLENN

*He was the first American to orbit Earth.*

## SPACE WALKS

Gagarin and Glenn remained in their capsules throughout their flights. The next stage in the space race was to see who would be the first to walk in space. The Soviets won but the United States followed a few months later with Gemini 4.

### VOSKHOD 2

*This 1965 Soviet mission saw Alexei Leonov make the first space walk. He stayed outside the craft for a full twelve minutes.*

GEMINI 4

# OTHER WORLDS

**W**ith space conquered, the next target was other planets. The nearest astral body to our planet is the Moon and in the second half of the 1960s both the United States and the Soviet Union planned to reach it first.

## MOON MISSIONS

In 1961, President John F. Kennedy said "We choose to go to the Moon." While the United States was not the first to reach the Moon, it was the first and only nation to land people on it. In 1959, the unmanned Soviet probe, Luna 1, made the first flyby of the Moon. Later that year another probe, Luna 2, landed on it. The Soviets sent several more probes to the Moon, putting some into orbit around it. In 1969, however, their achievements were topped by the United States when Apollo 11 landed on it.

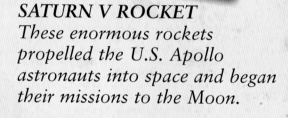

### SATURN V ROCKET
*These enormous rockets propelled the U.S. Apollo astronauts into space and began their missions to the Moon.*

### MOON WALKER
*The first man on the Moon was Neil Armstrong. He was followed by another eleven U.S. astronauts in six missions.*

### APOLLO CAPSULE
*This brought the Apollo astronauts back to Earth. After reentry, parachutes were deployed for a landing on water.*

**LUNOKHOD 1**
*The first roving spacecraft.*

## SPACE PROBES

Before and since the Moon landings, unmanned probes have been sent to other planets. Some have performed flyby missions, while others have landed and sent information about planetary surfaces back to Earth. In 1966, the Soviet craft Venera 3 was the first to place a probe on the surface of Venus.

**VIKING 2 LANDER**
*The U.S. Viking missions sent detailed images from the surface of Mars.*

**GALILEO**
*The probe Galileo, which visited Jupiter in 1995, was launched from a Space Shuttle.*

*SKYLAB*

## SPACE WORK

Space stations such as the U.S. Skylab have allowed astronauts to spend long periods of time in space and carry out scientific experiments. The Space Shuttle was developed partly to transport astronauts and materials to space stations.

**SHUTTLE ORBITER**
*The Space Shuttle orbiter lands on a runway like a plane. A parachute slows it down when it lands.*

# VOSTOK 1

Vostok 1 was the world's first manned spacecraft. It carried the Russian cosmonaut **Yuri Gagarin** into orbit around the Earth on April 12, 1961. Vostok 1 circled the Earth once before reentering the atmosphere. Gagarin ejected from the craft, 4.3 miles (7 kilometers) from the Earth's surface, gently descending into a field by parachute.

Gagarin ejected from the reentry module.

## VOSTOK REENTRY

*The reentry of Vostok 1 did not go as planned. After release, the reentry module remained attached to the rest of the spacecraft by a bundle of wires, only breaking away as these burned up. The reentry module spun wildly, but Gagarin ejected safely.*

Ejector hatch

Antenna

Yuri Gagarin

## REENTRY MODULE

This sphere was where Yuri Gagarin sat throughout the mission before he ejected. Upon reentry it broke away from the main body of Vostok 1.

Clamp bracket

Ejector seat

## RELEASE CLAMPS

During liftoff and orbit, release clamps held the reentry module tightly to the main body of Vostok 1. As the spacecraft descended towards Earth they were opened, but the reentry module remained attached by wires.

## EQUIPMENT MODULE

This contained the instruments for communicating with Earth and guiding the flight after the core stage rocket had fallen away. It also held the engine system for the final stage rocket.

### VOSTOK ROCKET

Vostok 1 — Vostok 1

*Vostok 1 was controlled from the ground. Four boosters propelled the craft from the Earth before burning out and falling away. The core stage rocket, which they had been attached to, took over and the capsule covering was released. When the core stage rocket burned out and fell away, the final stage rocket was ignited.*

Boosters

Stabilizing fins

### FINAL STAGE ROCKET

This pushed Vostok 1 into orbit after the large core stage rocket had fallen away. Once orbit was reached, it was discarded. A small retro engine on the underside of Vostok 1 directed its reentry.

Gas bottles

### ANTENNAE

During the flight, visual and radio signals were sent to **mission control** using these antennae.

## VOSTOK 1

**Length:** 23.8 feet (7.25 meters)
**Weight:** 5.2 tons
**Reentry module diameter:** 7.5 feet (2.3 meters)
**Maximum height above Earth:** 203 miles (327 kilometers)
**Time in orbit:** 108 minutes

# APOLLO COMMAND AND SERVICE MODULE

The Apollo missions took American astronauts to the Moon. The final descent was made by the lunar module but during the journey the astronauts traveled in the Command and Service Module (CSM). After the Apollo missions ended, NASA used the CSM in other missions.

## HEAT SHIELD

This side of the command module bore most of the friction as it reentered Earth's atmosphere. The heat shield prevented it from burning up.

Astronauts

Entry/escape hatch

## COMMAND MODULE

This is where the astronauts sat. One of them remained here while the others were on the Moon because he had to pilot the CSM during the docking of the lunar module.

Maneuvering thrusters

## DOCKING CLAMP

This is where the lunar module attached after returning from the Moon. The astronauts entered through a hatch in the middle of the clamp.

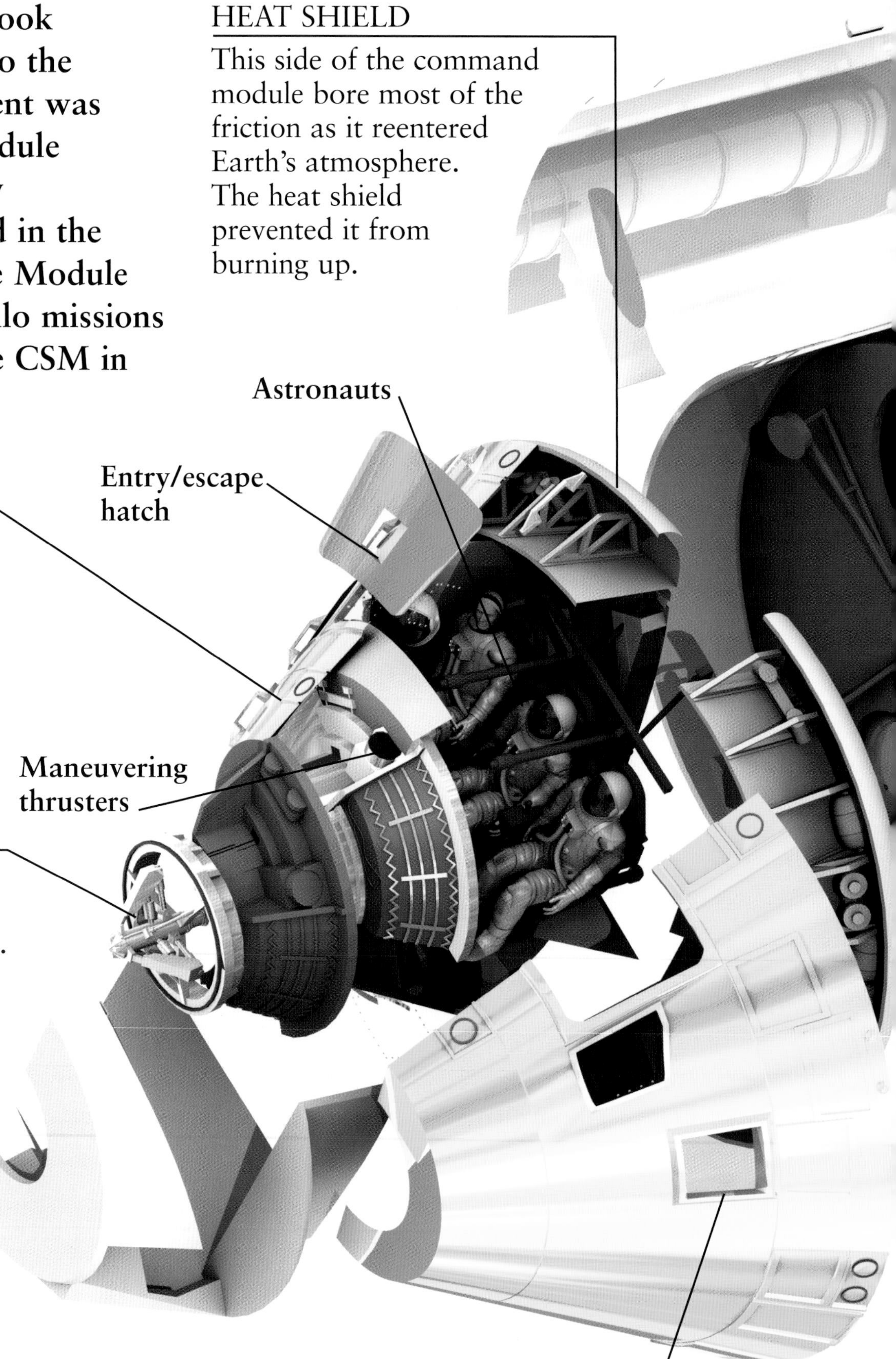

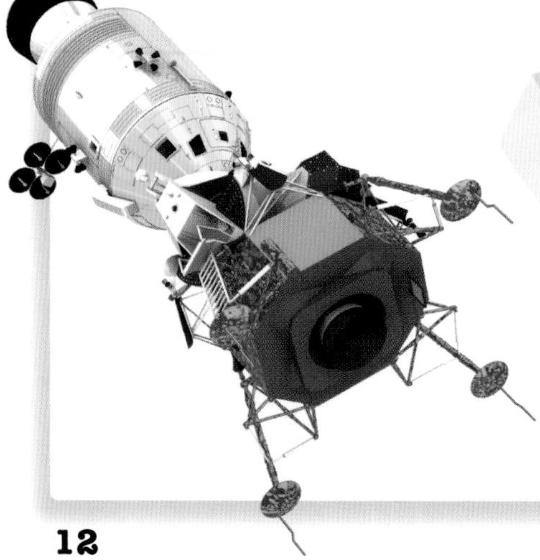

CSM docked with lunar module

Viewing window

## SERVICE MODULE ENGINE

This propelled the CSM into and out of lunar orbit. It also made midcourse corrections between the Moon and Earth. The engine used AeroZine 50 fuel—as did the lunar module.

## SATURN V ROCKET

*In order to propel a spacecraft to the Moon a huge amount of thrust was needed. That thrust was provided by the Saturn V rocket, which remains the most powerful launch vehicle ever used by NASA. With the Apollo spacecraft on top, the Saturn V was 364 feet (111 meters) high. It had three stages— essentially three separate rockets stacked on top of each other. Between them they used up more than 2,240 tons of fuel.*

Command module

Escape tower

Service module

Lunar module (stored)

Stage three

Stage two

Stage one

Main engines

## MANEUVERING THRUSTERS

These enabled the CSM to make small adjustments in its position. Their most important job was to align the CSM for docking with the lunar module.

## ANTENNA

The antenna allowed the astronauts to speak to the ground crew on Earth. It was folded flat during launch.

## APOLLO COMMAND AND SERVICE MODULE

**Length:** 36 feet (11 meters)
**Diameter:** 12.8 feet (3.9 meters)
**Weight:** 33.4 tons
**Crew cabin volume:** 219 square feet (6.2 cubic meters)
**Number of crew:** 3

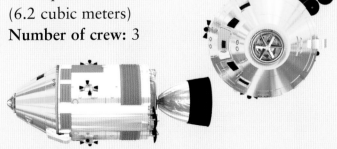

# APOLLO LUNAR MODULE

The Apollo lunar module was one of the most specialized vehicles ever built. Its job was to take astronauts from the Apollo Command and Service Module, orbiting the Moon, and transfer them to the Moon's surface. On the Moon, it provided living quarters for the astronauts for several days, before returning them to lunar orbit to join the Command and Service Module.

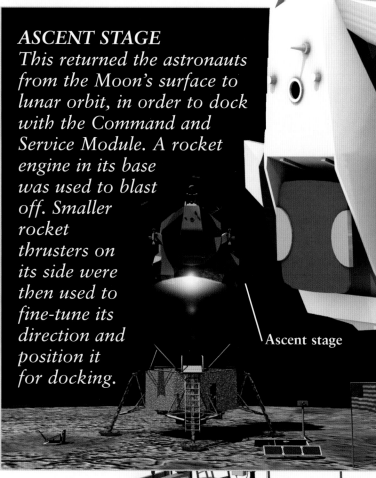

### ASCENT STAGE
*This returned the astronauts from the Moon's surface to lunar orbit, in order to dock with the Command and Service Module. A rocket engine in its base was used to blast off. Smaller rocket thrusters on its side were then used to fine-tune its direction and position it for docking.*

Ascent stage

Laser Ranging Retroreflector

Passive Seismic Experiment Package

### LUNAR SURFACE EXPERIMENTS
*Scientific experiments were carried out during the six Moon landings using equipment stored in the lander's descent stage. The Laser Ranging Retroreflector reflected a laser that was shone from Earth to measure the Moon's distance. The Passive Seismic Experiment Package detected "moonquakes."*

## APOLLO LUNAR MODULE
**Height:** 22.6 feet (6.9 meters)
**Weight (including fuel):** 16.8 tons
**Diameter:** 13.8 feet (4.2 meters)
**Crew cabin volume:** 235 square feet (6.65 cubic meters)
**Water storage capacity:** 50 gallons (190 liters)

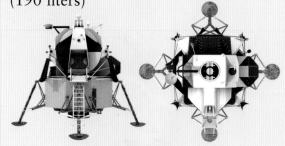

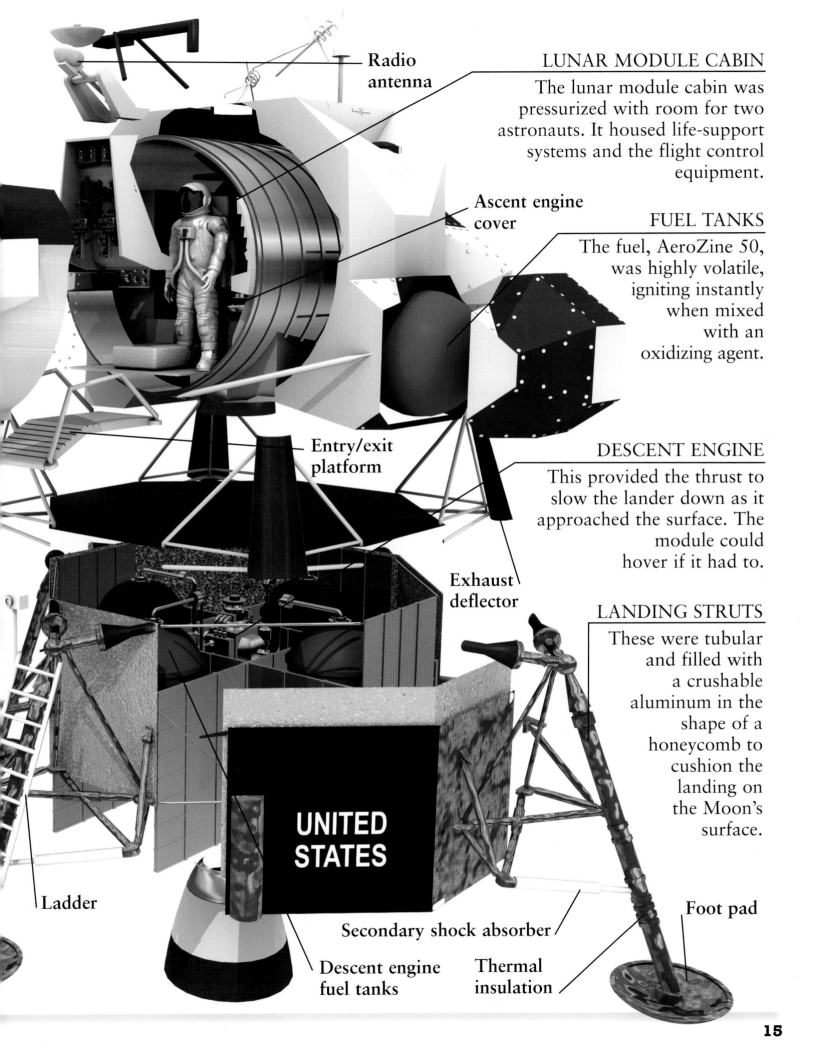

Radio antenna

## LUNAR MODULE CABIN
The lunar module cabin was pressurized with room for two astronauts. It housed life-support systems and the flight control equipment.

Ascent engine cover

## FUEL TANKS
The fuel, AeroZine 50, was highly volatile, igniting instantly when mixed with an oxidizing agent.

Entry/exit platform

## DESCENT ENGINE
This provided the thrust to slow the lander down as it approached the surface. The module could hover if it had to.

Exhaust deflector

## LANDING STRUTS
These were tubular and filled with a crushable aluminum in the shape of a honeycomb to cushion the landing on the Moon's surface.

UNITED STATES

Ladder

Secondary shock absorber

Foot pad

Descent engine fuel tanks

Thermal insulation

# LUNAR ROVER

The Lunar Rover was developed so that astronauts could travel farther during their three-day stays on the Moon. Lunar Rovers were used on the last three manned missions to the Moon: Apollo 15, Apollo 16, and Apollo 17. They traveled about 3 miles (5 kilometers) from the lunar module.

## CONTROLS

The Lunar Rover was controlled by a T-shaped joystick, pushed forward to accelerate, and moved left or right to steer. Pulling back on the joystick activated the brakes, unless a separate switch was pressed, which made the Lunar Rover reverse.

High-gain antenna

16 mm movie camera

Low-gain antenna

## COMMUNICATIONS

*The Lunar Rover carried several devices used to communicate with the Command and Service Module and Mission Control. The color TV camera was remotely operated by Mission Control on Earth. It was used not only to film excursions in the Lunar Rover but also filmed the module's takeoff and ascent at the end of the mission.*

Color TV camera

Communications relay unit

## POWER PACK

The Lunar Rover was a four-wheel-drive electric vehicle. It was powered by two 36-volt silver-zinc potassium hydroxide batteries.

Control console

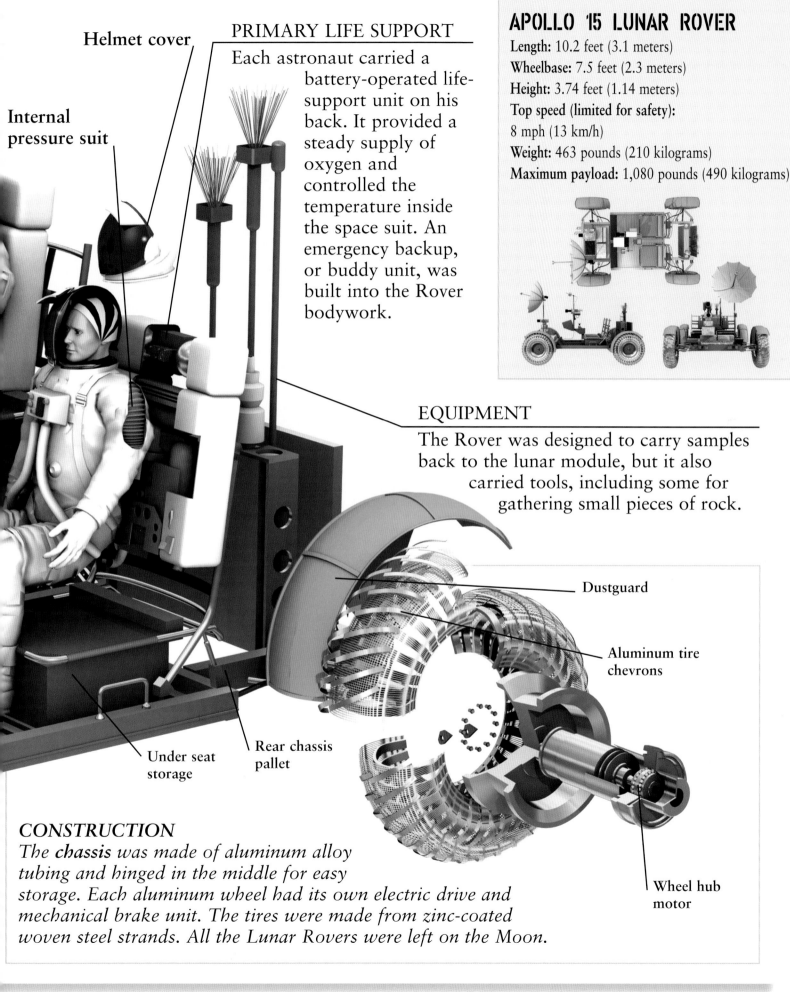

Helmet cover

Internal
pressure suit

## PRIMARY LIFE SUPPORT

Each astronaut carried a
battery-operated life-
support unit on his
back. It provided a
steady supply of
oxygen and
controlled the
temperature inside
the space suit. An
emergency backup,
or buddy unit, was
built into the Rover
bodywork.

### APOLLO 15 LUNAR ROVER

Length: 10.2 feet (3.1 meters)
Wheelbase: 7.5 feet (2.3 meters)
Height: 3.74 feet (1.14 meters)
Top speed (limited for safety):
8 mph (13 km/h)
Weight: 463 pounds (210 kilograms)
Maximum payload: 1,080 pounds (490 kilograms)

## EQUIPMENT

The Rover was designed to carry samples
back to the lunar module, but it also
carried tools, including some for
gathering small pieces of rock.

Dustguard

Aluminum tire
chevrons

Under seat
storage

Rear chassis
pallet

Wheel hub
motor

## CONSTRUCTION

*The **chassis** was made of aluminum alloy
tubing and hinged in the middle for easy
storage. Each aluminum wheel had its own electric drive and
mechanical brake unit. The tires were made from zinc-coated
woven steel strands. All the Lunar Rovers were left on the Moon.*

# SPACE SHUTTLE

The Space Shuttle was the first partially reusable spacecraft. It transported payloads into Earth's orbit, collected satellites from space and brought them back to Earth, and carried astronauts to and from the International Space Station. Six Space Shuttle orbiter vehicles were built. Five of them carried out missions in space.

## PAYLOAD BAY

This forms much of the length of the orbiter vehicle so the Space Shuttle can carry large objects into orbit. The **Hubble Space Telescope** was deployed in 1990 and has been visited five times by Space Shuttles since.

Antenna

Lens cover

Solar panels

Hubble Space Telescope

## ORBITER VEHICLE

This is the main reusable part of the Space Shuttle. As well as operating in space, the orbiter can glide and descend safely to a runway on the Earth's surface.

Main engines

Delta wings

## SHUTTLE ORBITER AND BOOSTER

**Total length:** 184 feet (56.1 meters)
**Total weight:** 2,274 tons
**Orbiter length:** 122 feet (37.2 meters)
**Orbiter wingspan:** 78 feet (23.8 meters)
**Operational altitude:**
115-621 miles (185-1,000 kilometers)
**Maximum payload:** 27.6 tons

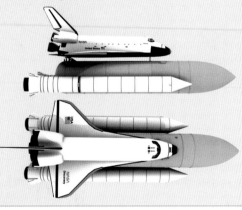

Liquid hydrogen

Solid fuel propellant

## ORBITER NOSE

*The front part of the orbiter vehicle houses the crew. An **air lock** hatch links it to a small chamber that opens out into the payload bay. In this chamber two astronauts can depressurize before a space walk. The nose is covered with heat-proof tiles that prevent the Orbiter from burning up as it reenters the Earth's atmosphere.*

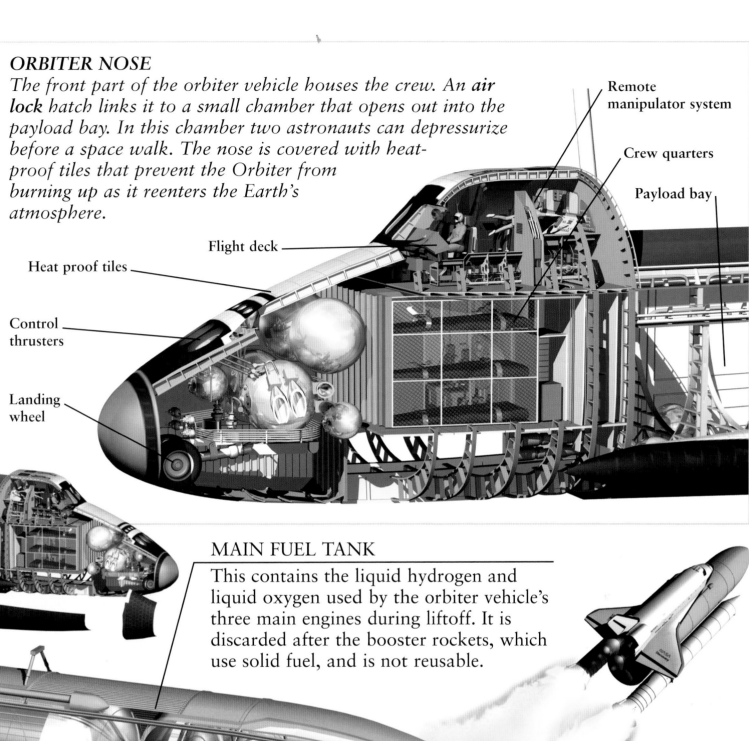

Remote manipulator system

Crew quarters

Payload bay

Flight deck

Heat proof tiles

Control thrusters

Landing wheel

## MAIN FUEL TANK

This contains the liquid hydrogen and liquid oxygen used by the orbiter vehicle's three main engines during liftoff. It is discarded after the booster rockets, which use solid fuel, and is not reusable.

**Shuttle at liftoff**

**Liquid oxygen**

**Parachutes**

## BOOSTER ROCKETS

These provide most of the thrust needed for liftoff. After launch they are discarded and descend by parachute to the sea, where they are recovered for reuse.

# MIR SPACE STATION

Mir was a Russian predecessor to the International Space Station. Its first section orbited the Earth beginning in 1986, where it was visited by two cosmonauts who shuttled across from Salyut-7—a smaller Russian space station, already in orbit. Its core was expanded upon, enabling Mir to operate for fifteen years. In 2001, it was brought out of orbit and crashed into the Pacific Ocean.

## SOLAR PANELS

These generated the electricity to power the life-support and other vital systems.

## MIR SPACE STATION

**Weight:** 1,392 tons
**Crew capacity:** 3
**Crew who worked on MIR:** 137
**Longest stay:** 438 days (by Valery Polyakov)
**Total time in orbit:** 5,511 days
**Date first occupied:** March 15, 1986
**Reentry:** March 23, 2001

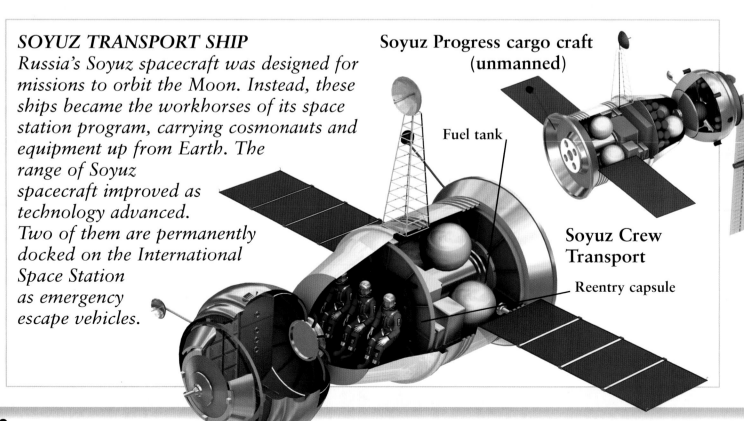

### SOYUZ TRANSPORT SHIP

*Russia's Soyuz spacecraft was designed for missions to orbit the Moon. Instead, these ships became the workhorses of its space station program, carrying cosmonauts and equipment up from Earth. The range of Soyuz spacecraft improved as technology advanced. Two of them are permanently docked on the International Space Station as emergency escape vehicles.*

Soyuz Progress cargo craft (unmanned)

Fuel tank

Soyuz Crew Transport

Reentry capsule

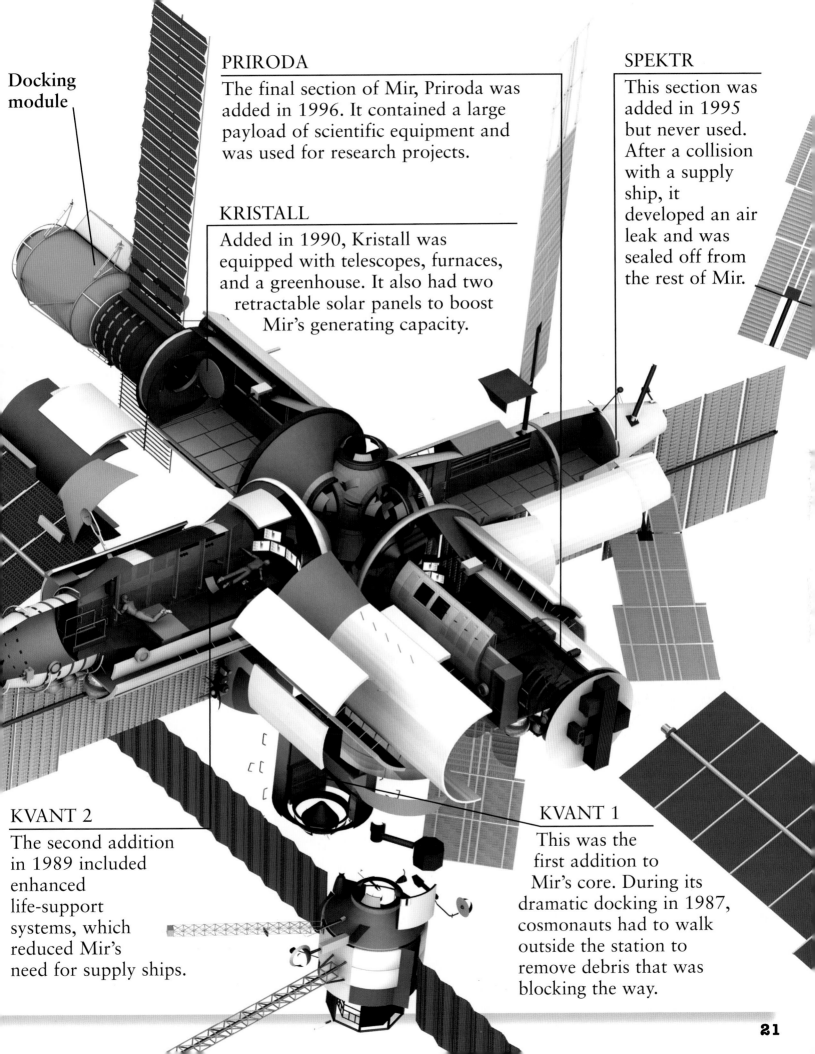

**Docking module**

## PRIRODA
The final section of Mir, Priroda was added in 1996. It contained a large payload of scientific equipment and was used for research projects.

## SPEKTR
This section was added in 1995 but never used. After a collision with a supply ship, it developed an air leak and was sealed off from the rest of Mir.

## KRISTALL
Added in 1990, Kristall was equipped with telescopes, furnaces, and a greenhouse. It also had two retractable solar panels to boost Mir's generating capacity.

## KVANT 2
The second addition in 1989 included enhanced life-support systems, which reduced Mir's need for supply ships.

## KVANT 1
This was the first addition to Mir's core. During its dramatic docking in 1987, cosmonauts had to walk outside the station to remove debris that was blocking the way.

# GPS SATELLITE AND LAUNCH ROCKET

Before Sputnik there were no artificial satellites around Earth. Today there are thousands, involved in everything from weather prediction to television broadcasting. GPS satellites were developed by the U.S. Department of Defense but are now used by everyone for navigation.

## ANTENNA ARRAY

Antenna **array** transmits a unique signal that can be detected by a GPS receiver. A receiver unit must pick up signals from at least three GPS satellites and use the times the signals took to reach it to calculate its position on Earth.

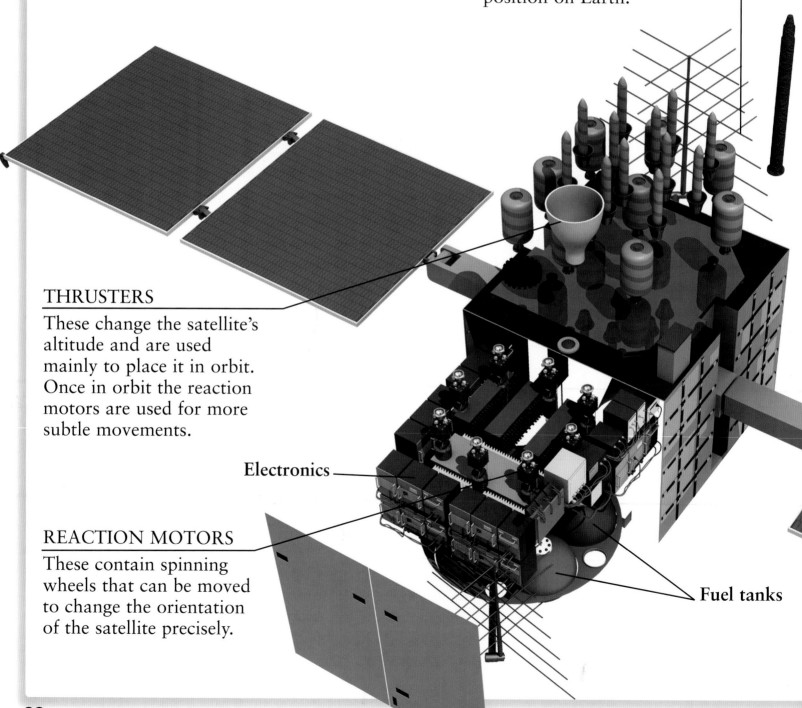

## THRUSTERS

These change the satellite's altitude and are used mainly to place it in orbit. Once in orbit the reaction motors are used for more subtle movements.

Electronics

## REACTION MOTORS

These contain spinning wheels that can be moved to change the orientation of the satellite precisely.

Fuel tanks

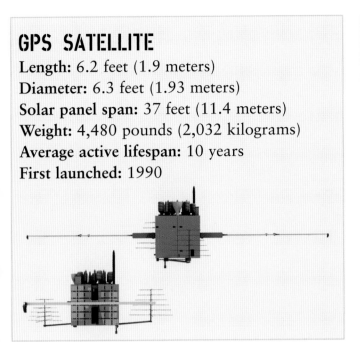

# GPS SATELLITE

**Length:** 6.2 feet (1.9 meters)
**Diameter:** 6.3 feet (1.93 meters)
**Solar panel span:** 37 feet (11.4 meters)
**Weight:** 4,480 pounds (2,032 kilograms)
**Average active lifespan:** 10 years
**First launched:** 1990

## SOLAR PANELS

These turn sunlight into electricity to power the satellite's systems. When the satellite is over the side of the Earth facing away from the Sun (at night) power is provided by rechargeable backup batteries.

**NAVSTAR GPS** satellite

Solar panels

Powered hinge

## SATELLITE LAUNCH VEHICLE

*The European Ariane four-rocket system takes communications and Earth observation satellites into space. Each Ariane rocket is only used once. When the fuel from the first stage has been used up, the second stage ignites to carry the payload into orbit. The payload can be up to 4.7 tons.*

Satellite payload stage

Second stage

First stage

**Ariane 4 rocket**

## SATELLITE TYPES

*GPS satellites circle the Earth several times a day. Many other satellites, including **communications satellites**, have geostationary orbits— orbits that rotate with the Earth in order to remain over the same place on its surface.*

**Communications satellite**

Antenna dish

# INTERNATIONAL SPACE STATION

## INTERNATIONAL SPACE STATION

**Length:** 356 feet (108.5 meters)
**Width:** 239 feet (73 meters)
**Weight:** 3,401 tons
**Average speed:** 17,239 mph (27,744 km/h)
**Crew capacity:** 6
**Average stay:** 6 months
**Main countries involved:** United States, Russia, Japan, Canada, Brazil, and ten European nations, including the United Kingdom, France, Germany, and Italy.
**Number of modules when complete:** 14

The International Space Station (ISS) orbits the Earth, circling our planet just over fifteen times a day, at an average height of 217 miles (350 kilometers) above the Earth's surface. It can be seen from the ground with the naked eye but a telescope or binoculars must be used to see any detail. Construction of the ISS in orbit began in 1998, with completion scheduled for 2011.

## ATV SUPPLY VEHICLE

The astronauts living on the ISS need regular supplies of food and equipment. Since 2008, these have been delivered by Automated Transfer Vehicles (ATV), such as the Jules Vernes ATV, developed by the European Space Agency (ESA).

**Jules Verne ATV**

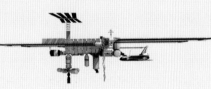

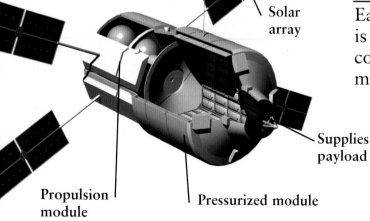

Solar array

Supplies payload

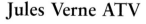
Propulsion module

Pressurized module

## SOLAR ARRAYS

Each of the four pairs of arrays is about 190 feet (58 meters) long and continually tilts in orbit to receive as much sunlight as possible.

**Radiator**

## MAIN TRUSS

The main **truss** forms the backbone of the ISS, providing the structure to which solar arrays, radiators, and other components are attached.

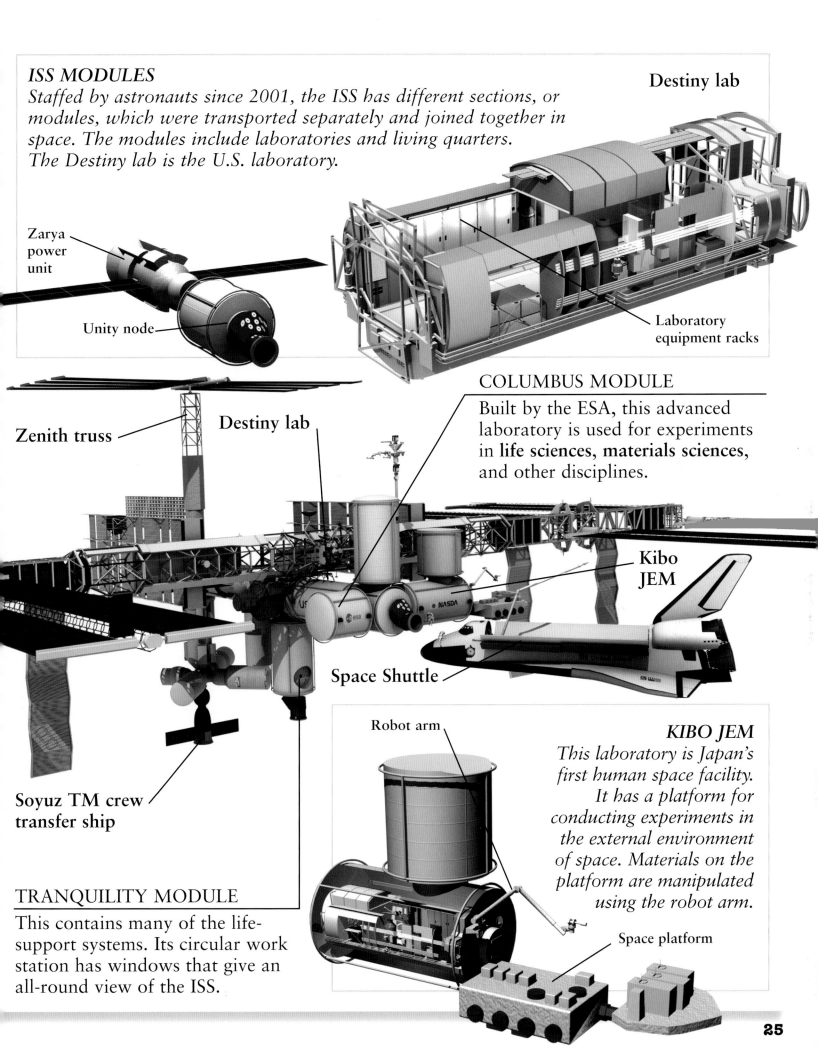

## ISS MODULES

*Staffed by astronauts since 2001, the ISS has different sections, or modules, which were transported separately and joined together in space. The modules include laboratories and living quarters. The Destiny lab is the U.S. laboratory.*

Destiny lab

Zarya power unit

Unity node

Laboratory equipment racks

Zenith truss

Destiny lab

## COLUMBUS MODULE

Built by the ESA, this advanced laboratory is used for experiments in **life sciences**, **materials sciences**, and other disciplines.

Kibo JEM

Space Shuttle

Soyuz TM crew transfer ship

## TRANQUILITY MODULE

This contains many of the life-support systems. Its circular work station has windows that give an all-round view of the ISS.

Robot arm

*KIBO JEM*
*This laboratory is Japan's first human space facility. It has a platform for conducting experiments in the external environment of space. Materials on the platform are manipulated using the robot arm.*

Space platform

25

# MARS ROVER

Panoramic cameras

The Mars Rover was designed by NASA to explore the surface of Mars. There have been three successful Mars Rover landings, the first of which was in 1997. Two more were landed in 2004 and were still working there in early 2010. The Mars Rover was partly inspired by the two Soviet Lunokhod rovers sent to the Moon in the 1970s.

## CAMERA MAST

This enables the Rover to "see" over rocks and other surface obstacles, making it easier to maneuver. The panoramic cameras also record landscape views.

## MARS EXPLORATION ROVER

**Length:** 5.2 feet (1.6 meters)
**Width:** 7.5 feet (2.3 meters)
**Height:** 4.9 feet (1.5 meters)
**Weight:** 408 pounds (185 kilograms)
**Top speed:** 1.9 inches (5 centimeters) per second
**Names:** Spirit (MER-A landed January 4, 2004), Opportunity (MERB landed January 25, 2004)

## SOLAR PANELS

These provide the Rover's electric power and recharge the batteries.

## *ROBOT TOOL ARM*

*This was designed to operate like a human arm. It has an "elbow," and a "wrist." The rock abrasion tool it carries does the same job as a geologist's hammer, exposing the insides of rocks. The microscopic imager provides magnifying views of the insides and outsides of rocks, and these are sent back to Earth for analysis.*

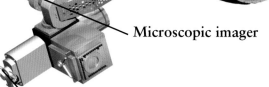

Microscopic imager

Rock abrasion tool

**Low-gain antenna**

## COMMUNICATIONS

The Mars Rover is remotely operated from Mission Control on Earth via the Mars Odyssey spacecraft, which orbits Mars. The high-gain antenna only transmits information and does not receive incoming signals.

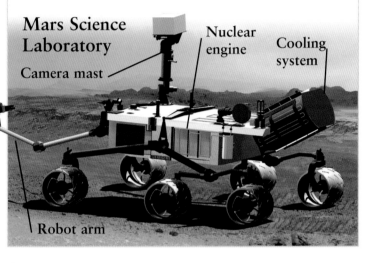

*FUTURE ROVER*
*The Mars Science Laboratory is a new rover scheduled to land on Mars in 2011. Five times heavier than the current Mars Rovers, it will carry ten times as much scientific equipment. Its main objective will be to find out whether life ever existed on Mars.*

**Mars Science Laboratory**

**Nuclear engine**

**Cooling system**

Camera mast

Robot arm

**High-gain antenna**

## ELECTRONICS BOX

This contains rechargeable batteries for power in low-light levels. The Rover is powered by its solar panels for at least four hours a day.

**Navigation camera**

**Gold foil insulation**

**Electric wheel motor**

## MOBILITY SYSTEM

The Mars Rover has six wheels mounted on a specialized suspension system, so that all of the wheels remain on the surface when driving over rough terrain. Each wheel has its own motor and rough treads to help with grip. The front and rear wheels steer the Rover.

# SpaceShipOne

SpaceShipOne is a relatively new development in space travel. On June 21, 2004, it became the first privately funded manned vehicle to enter space, flying just outside the Earth's atmosphere at an altitude of 62.7 miles (100.1 kilometers). Two more flights were made before SpaceShipOne was retired. During the third flight, it reached a maximum altitude of 69.5 miles (112 kilometers).

## *FLIGHT CONTROLS*

*SpaceShipOne's flight controls were similar to a jet fighter's controls. A joystick controlled lift and direction. Positioning information was sent via a digital display console, enabling the pilot to guide the spacecraft back to its landing site.*

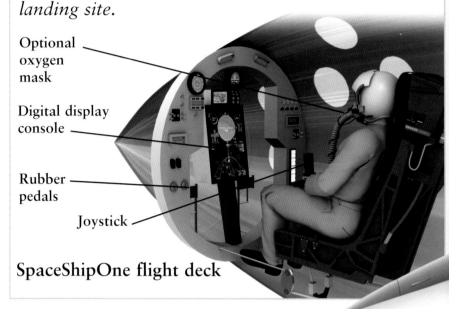

Optional oxygen mask

Digital display console

Rubber pedals

Joystick

SpaceShipOne flight deck

## FUSELAGE

Most of the **fuselage** housed the fuel tank and engine, but the cockpit was quite spacious. The nose cone was removed to let the pilot out.

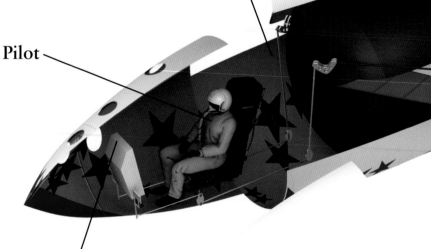

Pilot

Viewing ports

## SpaceShipOne

**Wingspan:** 16.4 feet (5 meters)
**Length:** 16.4 feet (5 meters)
**Weight:** 2,645 pounds (1,200 kilograms)
**Propellant:** Nitrous oxide and rubber hybrid rocket fuel
**Top speed:** 2,186 mph (3,518 km/h)
**Crew:** 1 (total capacity: 2)

## ROCKET MOTOR

This was ignited after the release of SpaceShipOne from White Knight. The pilot pulled SpaceShipOne into an almost vertical trajectory, flying through the edge of the atmosphere before switching off and gliding back down to land.

## WHITE KNIGHT MOTHER SHIP

*SpaceShipOne was launched at an altitude of 47,000 feet (14,326 meters) from beneath its mother ship, known as White Knight. The forward outer fuselage, cockpit, and* **avionics** *of White Knight were identical to those of SpaceShipOne. It was powered by turbojet engines rather than a rocket, and had two flight pilots.*

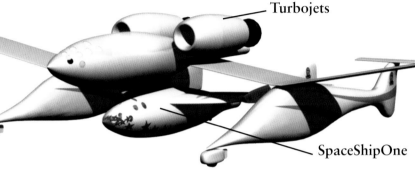

Turbojets

SpaceShipOne

**White Knight with SpaceShipOne**

Rudder

Nozzle

Aileron

## COMPOSITE SKIN

The outer skin was a graphite and epoxy composite material, combining lightness with strength.

**Wings in reentry position.**

## VARIABLE WINGS

The wings were designed to change position. During reentry their rear halves rotated to maximize resistance and slow down the craft.

# FUTURE MACHINES

Space exploration has only just begun. There are places in our own Solar System that probes have yet to visit. Future spacecraft will explore these, adding to our knowledge of the worlds that probes have visited already.

Scientists continue to work on strategies to send spacecraft to Mars, Jupiter, Jupiter's moons, and other worlds. NASA may return people to the Moon and build a sustainable base for astronauts to live on its surface. With the Space Shuttle shortly due to be retired, its replacement, the Orion spacecraft, is nearing the final stages of development.

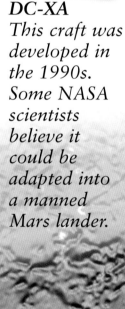

*DC-XA*
*This craft was developed in the 1990s. Some NASA scientists believe it could be adapted into a manned Mars lander.*

## MARS PHOENIX LANDER
*This craft reached Mars in 2008 and was the first to land in one of Mars' polar regions.*

## ORION CEV/MOON LANDER
*This lander is part of NASA's Constellation Project. The mission is to take explorers to the Moon and then onward to Mars and other planets.*

# GLOSSARY

**air lock**
An airtight chamber, usually between two areas of different air pressure. An air lock prevents a spacecraft's air from escaping, as it would if even a single door were opened.

**array**
A grouping or collection.

**astral body**
A planet or other large object in space.

**avionics**
An abbreviation of "aviation electronics," which are the electrical and electronic systems that enable an aircraft or similar vehicle to fly.

**chassis**
The rectangular steel frame that forms the basic skeleton of a motor vehicle. The axles and the frame that supports the bodywork are attached to the chassis.

**communications satellite**
An artificial satellite used for TV and radio broadcasting, telephone calls, computer links, and similar communications.

**cosmonaut**
An astronaut from Russia, or the former Soviet Union.

**fuselage**
The central body of an airplane or similar craft, to which the wings and tail are attached.

**Global Positioning System (GPS)**
A system of satellites that allows people with specialized receivers to pinpoint exactly where they are on the Earth.

**Hubble Space Telescope**
A large telescope that orbits the Earth.

**life sciences**
Sciences such as botany and zoology that study sliving things.

**material sciences**
Sciences such as applied physics and chemistry that study the properties of matter and its applications to engineering.

**Mission Control**
The hub on Earth, from which a space mission is monitored or controlled.

**moonquake**
A seismic event on the moon similar to an earthquake.

**National Aeronautics and Space Administration (NASA)**
The U.S. government agency responsible for the U.S. space program.

**payload**
The amount of people and material that a spacecraft can carry.

**reentry**
The return of a vehicle from space into the Earth's atmosphere.

**satellite**
An object that orbits, or circles, another object in space. The Moon is a natural satellite of Earth. Artificial satellites are those made by humans.

**Soviet Union**
A group of Communist countries that included Russia, East Germany, and Ukraine, among many others. The Soviet Union dissolved in 1991.

**space walk**
When astronauts in space put on space suits and go outside their spacecraft.

**truss**
An engineering term for a structure constructed with triangular units and straight beams that supports other structures.

**unity node**
A passageway that connects living and work areas in the International Space Station.

# INDEX